2/18

Backyard Bird Watchers

A Bird Watcher's Guide to
ORIOLES

By
Grace Elora

Gareth Stevens
PUBLISHING

Please visit our website, www.garethstevens.com. For a free color catalog of all our high-quality books, call toll free 1-800-542-2595 or fax 1-877-542-2596.

Cataloging-in-Publication Data

Names: Elora, Grace.
Title: A bird watcher's guide to orioles / Grace Elora.
Description: New York : Gareth Stevens Publishing, 2018. | Series: Backyard bird watchers | Includes index.
Identifiers: ISBN 9781538203279 (pbk.) | ISBN 9781538203293 (library bound) | ISBN 9781538203286 (6 pack)
Subjects: LCSH: Icterus (Birds)–Juvenile literature.
Classification: LCC QL696.P2475 E46 2018 | DDC 598.8'81–dc23

First Edition

Published in 2018 by
Gareth Stevens Publishing
111 East 14th Street, Suite 349
New York, NY 10003

Copyright © 2018 Gareth Stevens Publishing

Designer: Laura Bowen
Editor: Therese Shea

Photo credits: Cover, pp. 1 (oriole), 9 Gerald A. DeBoer/Shutterstock.com; cover, pp. 1–32 (paper texture) javarman/Shutterstock.com; cover, pp. 1–32 (footprints) pio3/Shutterstock.com; pp. 4–29 (note paper) totallyPic.com/Shutterstock.com; pp. 4–29 (photo frame, tape) mtkang/Shutterstock.com; pp. 5, 23 (top) Paul Reeves Photography/Shutterstock.com; p. 7 Linnette Engler/Shutterstock.com; p. 8 Mircea C/Shutterstock.com; p. 11 Gilles DeCruyenaere/Shutterstock.com; p. 13 Gerald Marella/Shutterstock.com; p. 15 Heather L. Hubbard/Shutterstock.com; p. 17 Steve Byland/Shutterstock.com; p. 19 George Grall/National Geographic/Getty Images; pp. 20, 27 (bird) Al Mueller/Shutterstock.com; p. 21 Juliancolton/Wikimedia Commons; p. 23 (bottom) G Fiume/Getty Images Sport/Getty Images; p. 25 (main) Robert L Kothenbeutel/Shutterstock.com; p. 25 (inset) Paul Sparks/Shutterstock.com; p. 26 Wilfred Marissen/Shutterstock.com; p. 29 (kids) FatCamera/E+/Getty Images; p. 29 (cookie) Tobik/Shutterstock.com.

Printed in the United States of America

CPSIA compliance information: Batch #CS17GS: For further information contact Gareth Stevens, New York, New York at 1-800-542-2595.

CONTENTS

Words in the glossary appear in **bold** type the first time they are used in the text.

ORANGE AND BLACK

Named After?

Both my city of Baltimore and the bird were named after the British Lord Baltimore who lived in the 1600s.

Hello! Welcome to my bird-watching guide! It's actually just me who will be reading it for now. I joined the Bird Buddies bird-watching club at my school. The teacher in charge—Ms. Avis—suggested we keep a journal so we remember things we want to tell each other every week. That's a good idea because I forget lots of things, like my homework!

The first few weeks of the club we're going to **focus** on an orange-and-black bird that lives around us called the Baltimore oriole.

Baltimore orioles really stand out among other birds because of their colors.

ORIOLE ABCS

Baltimore Oriole Wingspan

how wide wings are when spread = 12 inches (30 cm)

The Baltimore oriole is just one species, or kind, of oriole. There are about 30 oriole species in North and South America. There are orioles in Europe, Africa, Asia, and Australia, too.

Baltimore orioles are usually no longer than 8 inches (20 cm). They have long legs and a sharp beak. The male orioles are usually bright. They're black and orange or black and yellow. Females are duller colors. Both males and females have some white feathers on their wings, too.

Here's a female Baltimore oriole. She's a bit plainer, but still pretty!

FIELD TRIP

Oriole Calls
hew-li
cheh

Today, the Bird Buddies went to the park to look for orioles. They weren't easy to spot. The teacher said we were making too much noise. She said the birds are shy and might not come out if they could hear us.

We laid on blankets and were quiet for a while. Then, my friend JJ whispered that he saw something orange in the treetops. Ms. Avis said she heard the Baltimore oriole's song. I did, too. It sounded like a **flute**!

Baltimore orioles can be hard to spot—even with their bright colors.

WHAT'S GOOD TO EAT?

Nectar

Nectar is a sweet liquid that flowers make. It attracts bugs and birds such as orioles. These animals spread the flower's pollen so more flowers can grow.

I wondered if I could get Baltimore orioles to come to my backyard. We have a few bird feeders. I asked Ms. Avis what kind of birdseed I should buy. She helped me look up the answer on the Internet.

It turns out these orioles don't eat seeds. They mostly eat bugs and berries. They also eat some fruits that people eat, such as oranges, cherries, and grapes. The color of the food seems to matter. They like dark-colored fruits best!

People can make a sweet liquid with water and sugar to attract orioles, too! This feeder has a place for sugar-water <u>and</u> fruit.

11

ORANGE YOU GLAD, ORIOLE?

Things Orioles Eat

- grasshoppers
- wasps
- caterpillars
- beetles
- spiders
- snails
- berries
- fruits

We had an orange at home, so I cut it and put it in the feeder. Take a look at the photo I took on the next page. I can't wait to show it to the club!

The oriole ate the orange in a weird way. It stuck its closed beak into the orange. Then the oriole opened its beak, cutting the fruit. The bird used its tongue to lick the orange juice. I don't think Mom would like it if I drank my juice like that!

Look who I found eating the orange!

13

THEY NEED TREES!

Nests Are Made of:

bark, grass, grapevines, yarn, string, moss, hair, plant matter

Some kinds of birds are endangered. That means they're in danger of dying out! Baltimore orioles aren't endangered. But their homes are. Many live in tall trees called American elms. Dutch elm **disease** is killing many of these beautiful trees.

Luckily, Baltimore orioles can make their nests in other kinds of tall trees. They like trees with lots of leaves to hide them and their nests. Their nests are strange. They look like a bag made of plant parts hanging off a branch!

14

The oriole nest looks like it might fall, doesn't it?

LOOK UP, WAY UP!

How a Male
Asks, "Will You
Be My Mate?"

1. faces female

2. stretches up

3. bows and
spreads wings

The female oriole builds a nest
in the spring, with some help from
the male. They're **mates**. That means
they're going to have a family.

The nest is usually built in a
tall tree, at the end of the branch.
It's often about 25 feet (8 m) off the
ground. That's like five of my friends
standing on top of each other! A
nest high off the ground is safer from
animals that would eat the orioles,
such as cats.

Here's a female getting string for her nest.

TENDING THE EGGS

Oriole Enemies

cats

squirrels

large birds

The mother oriole usually lays four or five eggs at a time. Ms. Avis brought in a broken oriole eggshell. It was bluish. Some oriole eggs are gray. It's easy to tell Baltimore oriole eggs from others. They have brown or black marks on one end.

I know the eggs have to be kept warm the whole time. That's called incubation. The mother sits on the eggs for 2 weeks. The father stays nearby and may sing special alarm calls to scare off enemies.

A father oriole guards the nest and watches for danger.

19

FROM NESTLING TO FLEDGLING

When the oriole chicks **hatch**, they're called nestlings. That's not hard to remember! But they're only nestlings for about 2 weeks. During that time, both the mother and father are very busy feeding them.

When the birds leave the nest, they're called fledglings. They hop and flutter while learning to fly. They still get food from their parents. When they get good enough at flying and finding food, they go off by themselves. That's like my older brother going off to college!

Here's a picture of a nestling. It's hoping for food!

21

PLAY BALL!

That's a Big Chick!

On April 6, 1979, the Oriole mascot hatched out of a giant egg at Memorial Stadium in Baltimore!

Guess what? Mom got us two tickets for the baseball game. I got to meet our team's **mascot**—a Baltimore oriole. It was so funny! Our team won, too!

My city, Baltimore, is in Maryland. The Baltimore oriole is the state bird of Maryland. That's why the baseball team here named themselves the Baltimore Orioles. The team also chose colors for their **uniforms** that are a bit like the bird's colors: orange, black, and white.

I don't think the mascot looks much like a real oriole, but it was really funny!

LOOK-ALIKES

Helpers!
Baltimore orioles eat caterpillars that can do harm to trees!

At the club today, Ms. Avis had many photos of other kinds of orioles. They look different from Baltimore orioles.

She said that Baltimore orioles and Bullock's orioles were once both called northern orioles. However, scientists discovered that they're different species. They live in different places, too. Bullock's orioles live in the western part of the United States and Baltimore orioles live in the East. These birds live together in areas around the center of the United States. They even mate with each other.

Bullock's oriole

Baltimore oriole

Can you see how these two birds look alike, but also different? Male Bullock's orioles have a black line through their eye.

FREQUENT FLIERS

It would be hard for an oriole to hide in snow all winter, so I'm glad they go south.

Baltimore orioles don't like the cold weather. They start **migrating** as early as July. They fly south, as far as Florida, Central America, and even South America. That's a very long way!

They'll be back in April to mate and have a family again. They can live to be 10 years old, so they do the journey back and forth a few times. Next year, I'll be ready with oranges and grape jelly for them!

BALTIMORE ORIOLE MIGRATION MAP

North
America

Take a look where
Baltimore orioles
live in summer
and winter.

- summer
- winter

South
America

ADIOS, ORIOLES!

Today was the last day of watching Baltimore orioles with the club. We **celebrated** with a party. I brought in bird cookies that I made with Grandpa. We filled a huge **poster** with all the facts we learned about this cool bird. It's a good thing we had these journals to help us!

Ms. Avis told us to keep the journals. We could write books about birds someday with all our **research**. What bird will we study next?

I learned a lot in the bird-watching club—and made friends, too!

GLOSSARY

attract: to cause something to like or be interested in something

celebrate: to do something special for an event

disease: an illness

flute: a musical instrument shaped like a thin pipe and played by blowing across a hole near one end

focus: to direct your attention or effort at something

hatch: to come out of an egg

mascot: a person, animal, or object used to represent a group such as a sports team

mate: one of two animals that come together to make babies. Also, to come together to make babies.

migrate: to move to warmer or colder places for a season

pollen: a fine yellow dust produced by plants

poster: a large sheet of paper

research: careful study that is done to find out something new

uniform: a special kind of clothing that is worn by all the members of a team

FOR MORE INFORMATION

Books

Boring, Mel. *Birds, Nests, and Eggs.* Louisville, CO: NorthWord Press, 2014.

Cuddy, Robbin. *Learn to Draw Birds & Butterflies: Step-by-Step Instructions for More Than 25 Winged Creatures.* Minneapolis, MN: Lerner Publisher Services, 2016.

Elliott, David. *On the Wing.* Somerville, MA: Candlewick Press, 2014.

Websites

Baltimore Oriole
www.allaboutbirds.org/guide/baltimore_oriole/lifehistory
Read some more tips about bringing orioles to your yard.

Baltimore Oriole
www.audubon.org/field-guide/bird/baltimore-oriole
This is a great site to hear the songs and calls of this bird.

INDEX